About this book

Kelly is excited it is finally time for her COVID-19 vaccine. Her little brother Joey is not so sure he wants a shot. Their mom, a doctor, explains ... development, biology, and history. Kelly and Joey learn ... works, what to expect, and how the vaccine will help us ... Lauren Block MD MPH, a physician, and Adam E. Block Ph... help parents explain scientific principles behind coronavirus and vaccination to their kids.

AFTER CORONAVIRUS

AFTER VACCINE

Kelly Gets a Vaccine: How We Beat Coronavirus

Copyright © 2020 by Lauren Block, MD MPH and Adam E. Block, PhD

All rights reserved. No part of this publication may be reproduced, distributed or transmitted in any form or by any means, including photocopying, recording, or other electronic or mechanical methods, without the prior written permission of the publisher, except in the case of brief quotations embodied in critical reviews and certain other noncommercial uses permitted by copyright law.

Illustrated by Debby Rahmalia
www.instagram.com/debbyrahmalia

Blockstar Publications
www.kellygetsavaccine.com
Available on Amazon and at other book retailers

ISBN: 978-1-7349493-9-1 (soft cover)

Lauren D. Block MD MPH and Adam E. Block PhD
Illustrations by Debby Rahmalia
Email: coronaviruschildrensbook@gmail.com

1. Juvenile fiction
2. Health & Daily Living——Diseases, Illnesses and Injuries ——United States of America with int. Distribution.

Photo of author Dr. Lauren Block receiving the COVID-19 vaccine on December 19, 2020.

"...an you believe we are finally getting ... COVID-19 vaccine?" Kelly asks.
"...e are," says Mom. "We are going to ... pediatrician's office today."
...ey is worried. He does not like shots.
...t he has a plan. He is not going to let
...one give him a shot.

1

"How does the vaccine work?" Kelly asks.

"Vaccines trick our bodies into thinking we have already been infected, so we develop antibodies to protect ag[...]
illness if we do get exposed to a virus," Mom says.

"Like an antibody test?" asks Kelly.

"That is exactly right," says mom. "People who have had the virus make antibodies, which protect us in case w[...]
the virus again. Some of these people had symptoms and some were asymptomatic, or symptom-free. People [...]
have had the vaccine also make antibodies which protect against infection. Come, let's get in the car."

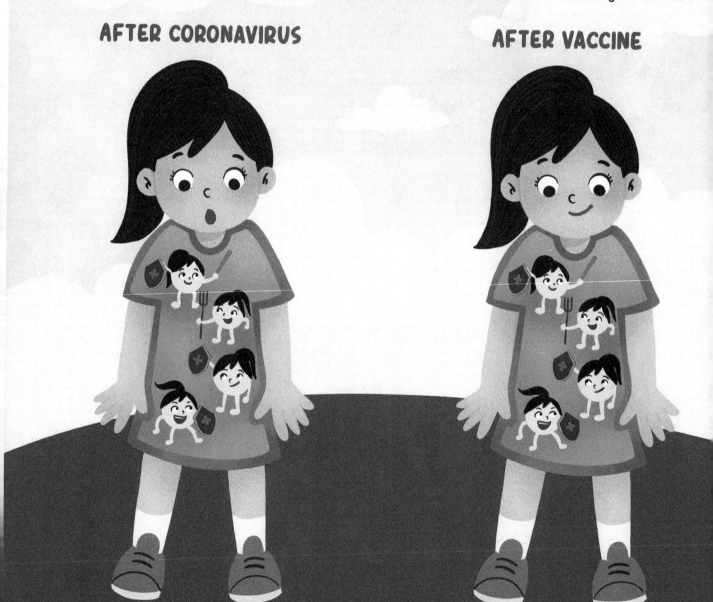

AFTER CORONAVIRUS

AFTER VACCINE

"Do vaccines really work?" Joey asks. "Yes. Vaccines have saved countless lives. Vaccines work so well that several terrible diseases have been eliminated or close to eliminated. Smallpox was an awful illness that has been completely eradicated, or eliminated from circulation. When Grandma was little, kids got really sick from polio until a vaccine came out. Parents took their children to wait in line for hours to get the vaccine. And now every child gets the vaccine. Look, we're here!"

HOSPITAL

"Did I get the polio vaccine, Mom?" Kelly asks.
"Yes, you both did. You got your first vaccines when you were just born and only weighed 7 pounds! You got vaccines against hepatitis, polio, measles, rubella, and others. These are standard and required for school, so all kids usually get the same vaccines."

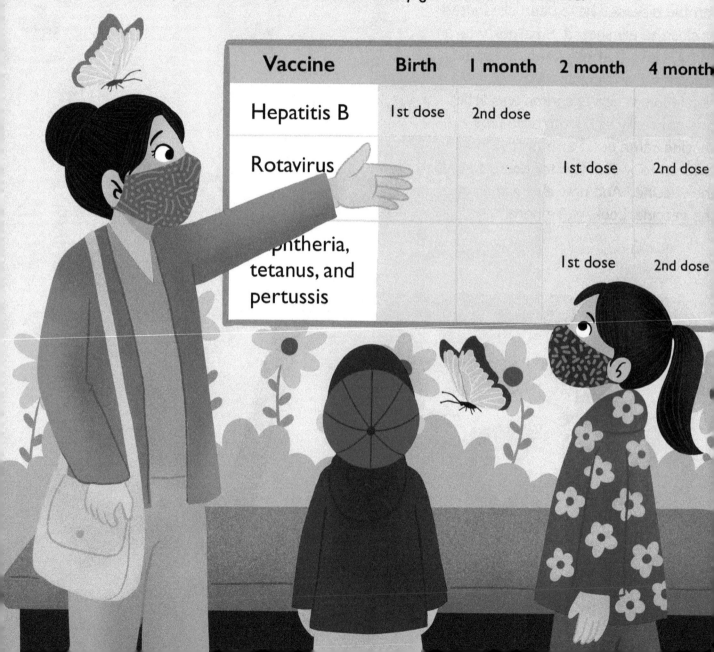

Vaccine	Birth	1 month	2 month	4 month
Hepatitis B	1st dose	2nd dose		
Rotavirus			1st dose	2nd dose
Diphtheria, tetanus, and pertussis			1st dose	2nd dose

"No fair, grown-ups don't need to get any shots," Joey says. "Grown-ups got these vaccines when we were kids. Or worse. I got chicken pox when I was five. I was itchy all over for my fifth birthday. Now you get a shot and you will never get chicken pox! The chicken pox vaccine you get as a child may last your whole life. But other vaccines, like the flu shot, only last a few months or a year. So adults and kids get the flu shot every year."

Get Your
Flu Shot
Every
Winter !

"So we need to get this COVID shot every year?" whines Joey. He is still not planning to get the shot.

"Maybe," says Mom. "We do not know yet how long immunity, or antibodies, will last following the vaccine. It may be a year, or two years, and another vaccine might be needed. Some vaccines are only needed once in a lifetime, but others only last about a year."

"Why has it taken SO LONG to make the coronavirus vaccine?" asks Kelly. "I feel like we've been waiting forever!"
"Actually, most vaccines take ten years or more to make. Scientists around the world worked together and were able to make the COVID-19 vaccine in less than ONE year. Governments across the world, from China to Russia to Europe to the US, gave money to help scientists develop a vaccine."

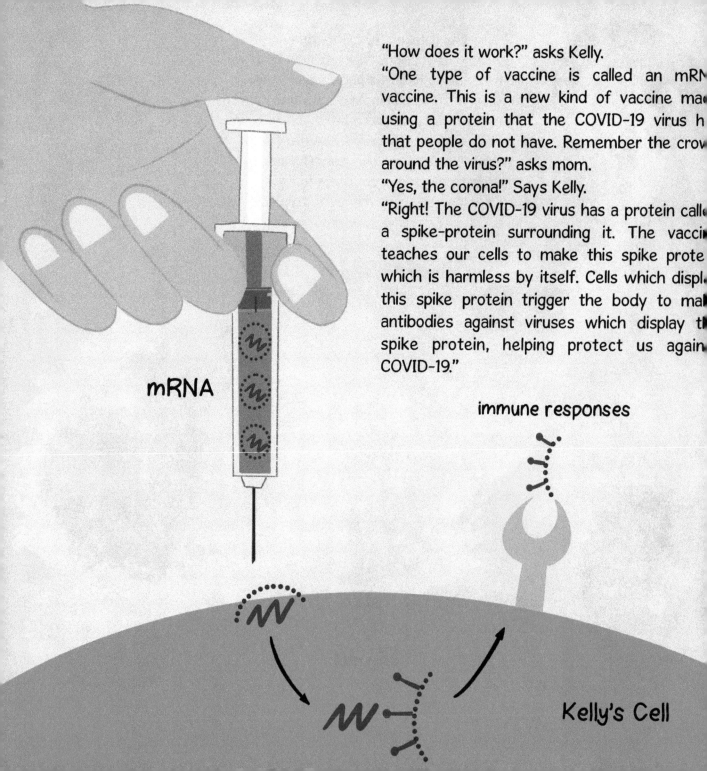

"How does it work?" asks Kelly.

"One type of vaccine is called an mRN[A] vaccine. This is a new kind of vaccine mad[e] using a protein that the COVID-19 virus h[as] that people do not have. Remember the crow[n] around the virus?" asks mom.

"Yes, the corona!" Says Kelly.

"Right! The COVID-19 virus has a protein call[ed] a spike-protein surrounding it. The vacci[ne] teaches our cells to make this spike prote[in] which is harmless by itself. Cells which displ[ay] this spike protein trigger the body to ma[ke] antibodies against viruses which display t[he] spike protein, helping protect us again[st] COVID-19."

mRNA

immune responses

Kelly's Cell

"Another vaccine was created in a totally different way. The other one uses a harmless virus, called a viral vector. This is combined with pieces of the COVID-19 virus inserted into it. Once inside human cells, these cells begin to make COVID-19 proteins. And these proteins trigger an antibody response just like the mRNA vaccines."

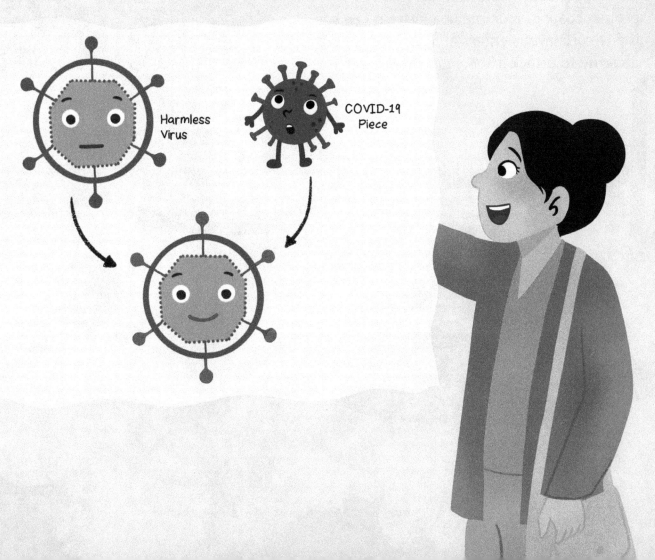

Harmless Virus

COVID-19 Piece

"They inject you with a virus? I thought we were trying to avoid the virus?" exclaims Joey in disbelief.

"We are, Joey. But the small piece of virus you are injected with is harmless. It tricks your cells to make the outside coating of the coronavirus without the rest of the virus. Once your body makes the coronavirus protein coating, your immune system can see if any coronavirus enters and has already built an army to attack it."

"How do we REALLY know this vaccine works?" asks Joey, who still really didn't want to get a shot.

"We know these vaccines work well in the studies, which is called efficacy. Scientists design clinical trials, which are tests of whether the vaccines work in thousands of people. Brave volunteers sign up to participate in these trials. Phase 1 trials are small trials done to see if the vaccine is safe and what dose to use. Phase 2 trials are slightly larger and done to see if the vaccine is effective."

"So then the vaccine comes out?" Kelly bursts in.
"There are a few more steps," explains mom. "Phase 3 trials are the largest and done at several different hospitals or offices. These last longer and compare the vaccine to a placebo, or fake vaccine that looks like the real vaccine. Both people and the scientists don't know who gets the real vaccine and who gets the fake. Then the scientists wait and see how many people who got the vaccine get sick and how many people who got the placebo get sick."

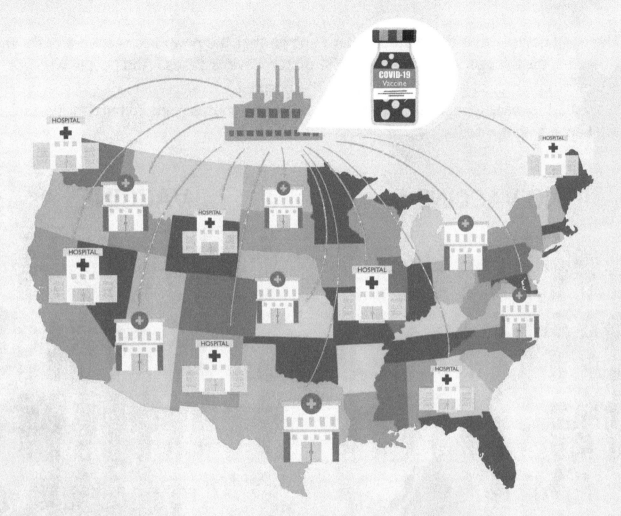

"So then the vaccine FINALLY comes out?" asks Kelly.

"Almost," says mom. "The government works closely with the company during these trials. All the information is made available to the public. If the vaccine passes the phase 1, 2, and 3 trials, a part of the government called the Food and Drug Administration, or FDA, will approve the vaccine. In the case of COVID-19, because everyone wants this vaccine as soon as possible, the FDA gives emergency approval for the vaccine. But they keep watching for other developments and side effects after the vaccine comes out."

"And then?" urges Kelly.

"Then the drug company, with the government's help, has to make enough of the vaccine to get to people throughout the country, and doctors and nurses have to figure out how to give the vaccine to their patients. This can take months."

"The good news is that these studies have shown that the new vaccines work really well. In the studies, the vaccines prevented 95% of coronavirus cases. And people who got coronavirus were less likely to die or go to the hospital."

"Wow, that is really effective!" says Kelly. "I know the shot is going to hurt a little, but I am happy to get it today."

NO VACCINE

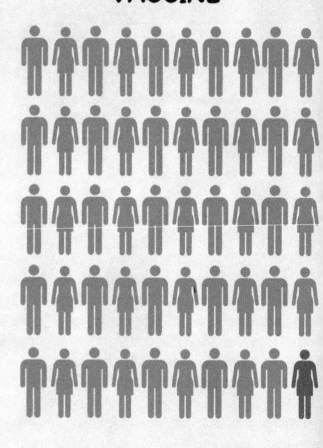

VACCINE

without covid

with covid

t doesn't hurt very much, Kelly," says her mom. "I got my first dose a month ago and just got
y second dose this month. My arm hurt a little for a few days and I felt chills the day after,
ut otherwise, I'm fine. We can relax at home if you don't feel well tomorrow."

You had to get the shot twice?" exclaims Joey. There was no way he was getting two shots.

Yes. This is a two-dose vaccine. Like many vaccines, two shots 3-4 weeks apart are needed to
event future infection. You become immune, or protected, one week after the second shot."

MRNA CORONAVIRUS VACCINE

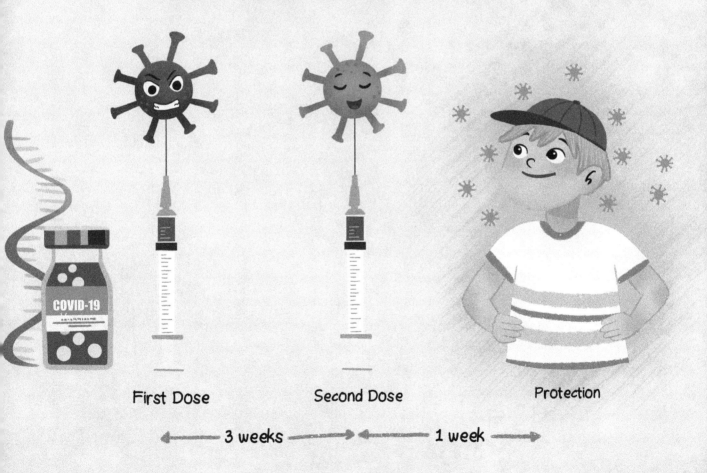

First Dose   Second Dose   Protection

← 3 weeks →   ← 1 week →

"No fair, why did you get it first?" asked Kelly.
"Physicians and other health care workers got it first because we are exposed to people with coronavirus every day as part of our jobs helping people who are sick. Many doctors, nurses and other clinical workers have gotten sick and some even died helping treat others for coronavirus. Older and high risk people also got the shot first".

hat didn't hurt too much," Kelly says after getting the shot. "Now I can go back to camp, vacation, d birthday parties!"

t so fast, kiddo. We won a battle against coronavirus today, but the war is not over. It will take time us to beat coronavirus. Getting an effective vaccine is a big step, but coronavirus does not end the cond you get the vaccine. How well the vaccine works in the real world depends on how many people t the vaccine, and how well the vaccine works in a range of people. This is called effectiveness."

"Joey, are you ready for your shot?" his mom asks.
"I'm not getting it. I don't care if I get sick!" Joey says.
"You know getting a shot doesn't just help you. You are also doing it to help others."
"I am?" asks Joey.
"Yes," says mom. "Everyone who gets vaccinated helps promote herd immunity."

'erd immunity means that when most people are
mmune, the virus cannot spread widely. Scientists believe
/e need 70% immune to reach herd immunity. So, if the
accine is 90% effective, and 80% of people get the
accine, we will have (80% x 90%) = 72% immunity.
"his is about enough needed to reach herd immunity".

"Great, so I don't need to get it. I can be one of the 20% of people who don't get it," Joey says, triumphantly. "Some people may not be able to get vaccines due to illnesses or medications they take which weaken their immune system. People who can't get the vaccine, including kids who have cancer or other diseases, are depending on you, Joey to get the vaccine like Kelly did, so we get to herd immunity to protect everyone."

"So if I get it, it will help kids who can't get the vaccine?" says Joey.

"Yes, getting vaccinations is something everyone can do to help people who are too sick to be able to take a vaccine or do not have access to the vaccine."

"I'll do it," Joey says proudly.

"My friend Erica says her parents won't let her get the sh
She said vaccines are too risky."

"Every parent is different and every parent gets to choos
whether their family gets the vaccine. Some people are
hesitant, or afraid of potential side effects. However, the
science behind vaccines is clear. Vaccines are safe and kid
who get vaccines are healthier than kids who do not."

"Does it cost a lot of money?" asks Kelly.

"No, the government has paid for the vaccine to be affordable for Americans. The vaccine is covered by insurance and available for a small fee for people who do not have insurance. Some other countries will also have the vaccine widely available, but in other countries it may be harder for some people to get the vaccine."

"What about people who still get sick?" asks Kelly.
"Some people will still get sick, probably for a long time. Thankfully doctors and other healthcare providers now know treatments that work better for really sick patients. Steroid medicines prevent the immune system from attacking organs in the body. New antibody treatments help give people antibodies once they get sick to prevent serious complications from the infection. We keep getting better at treating people who get sick."

"So then can we get back to normal?" asks Joey. "By my birthday in May?"
"Once we are all able to get the vaccine, we can start to get closer to normal. Schools and businesses can start to re-open. Masks will be part of our lives for some time. We will also need to continue to keep our distance, wash our hands, and avoid big crowds. It will probably take a long time before we can get back to big parties. But since you two got the vaccine today, we are one step closer to beating coronavirus."

CPSIA information can be obtained
at www.ICGtesting.com
Printed in the USA
LVHW060749310122
709584LV00020B/26